THE PORTFOLIO SECRETS

Cracking the Code of
18 Product Design Portfolios

Xinran Ma

Cover design by Xinran Ma
Cover image by jozefmicic/Adobe Stock

ISBN: 9798322275992

For Rufei, Amelia, and Olivia

CONTENTS

INTRODUCTION

I didn't want to write a book about portfolios.

Over the past ten years, there have been countless articles, social media posts, presentations, and discussions about portfolios. Enough has been said.

It is also the topic I get asked about the most during my mentorship sessions. I'm used to jumping on a video call to review portfolios.

That's why, when I was writing my first two books, *The Minimalist Career Changer* and *Case Study Storytelling*, I didn't focus too much on portfolios.

I believed that other topics related to product design or UX were more meaningful for me to share.

Until one day, I changed my mind.

It was a Thursday night. Someone I had never met before booked a mentorship session with me. She sent me the link to her portfolio in the chat and asked for feedback. I opened the link.

Upon landing on the homepage, I glanced at it and then clicked on the first case study for another quick look.

I frowned. The portfolio needed a lot of work.

If I were the hiring manager, I would move on to the next applicant's portfolio and not consider her as a candidate.

However, I didn't tell her this. I didn't want to discourage her because it was apparent she had invested considerable effort into her portfolio. She was also proud of it.

Many issues in her portfolio related to the design quality of both the website and UI. The first impression was not good. Although I knew these were not the only criteria to evaluate a portfolio.

She tried to showcase her thought process and tell a story in her case studies. However, without a strong first impression, hiring managers might not even proceed to read her portfolio further. In this competitive job market, they had more than enough portfolios to review.

So, I recommended a few areas for improvement at a high level. I didn't want to delve into granular details, although they were important.

"What do you mean?" she looked baffled. "Do you mean my portfolio is not good enough?"

I stuttered.

I acknowledged the strengths of her portfolio and her effort in putting it together, then hesitantly pointed out more areas that needed improvement.

I knew it was a rabbit hole and that delving too deeply wouldn't be the best use of our time during a short video call.

Before I realized it, the meeting had already gone over. I had to ask her to feel free to schedule another session with me.

I ended the meeting feeling unsettled.

That session was unlike my other video calls, where I ensured attendees received what they looked for with enough actionable insights. That time, it felt as though I had opened Pandora's box, leading to even more confusion and discouragement for her.

I wish I could have been more helpful.

I wish I could have explained more by pulling out some good examples and pointing to them as references.

I wish I could have told her that great portfolios look great because of some small, common details.

Great designers don't often share those granular details. It's not that they don't want to; they've simply internalized them as part of their craft, making them second nature.

However, for other designers, those small details can make a significant difference in the first impression.

If these insights could even be called "secrets", then I wanted to uncover and share them with the people who need them.

That was the moment I decided to write this book.

$$\sim$$

WHO THIS BOOK IS FOR

If you are a career changer trying to break into product design or UX, this book is particularly helpful for you. It delves into common tips in depth while providing other insights that are not often seen elsewhere. The carefully selected examples in this book can fast-track your progress to a portfolio that catches the attention of hiring managers and helps you secure more interviews.

If you are a junior or mid-level product designer already working in the field, this book can elevate your portfolio to a new level. You may be familiar with many of the points covered in this book, but it offers insights on a deeper level, and you can use the detailed data in the second part as references.

If you are a senior product designer or manager, this book can serve as a refresher on some familiar topics. I have tried to break down complex concepts into small, digestible chunks. I hope this book can help you share these insights with other designers who could benefit from them.

~

HOW I SELECTED THOSE PORTFOLIOS

I took the selection process seriously. What you use as inspiration determines how high you can achieve.

Here is what the process looked like.

The Initial Screening

I screened over two hundred good portfolios from the internet:

- Most of them were from selective portfolio showcase websites like Bestfolio.
- Some were from my bookmarks collected over the years.
- Others came from recommendations by other designers.

The Further Screening

I narrowed down the selection to eighteen portfolios based on the following criteria:

1) Relevancy

Some portfolios were good inspirations but no longer relevant in today's context, so I filtered them out. I also filtered out portfolios that focused more on brand design than on product design.

2) Learnability

Some portfolios were outliers; they were either too unique or too complex for other designers to use as references. Some portfolios required passwords to access most case studies. Some portfolios were overly simplistic, including minimal information about their projects—effective enough for some senior design leaders but not sufficiently helpful for most designers. I filtered out all of them.

3) Variety

It is important to include portfolios with different styles. After all, there is no one-size-fits-all standard. For example, I ensured some portfolios excelled in visuals, and others in storytelling; some were classic portfolios from design leaders, while others were from emerging designers.

The Final Screening

There were twenty-five portfolios in the final round. I further narrowed it down to eighteen by removing some that were similar. Given the overwhelming amount of portfolio examples available online, I wanted to include the featured ones instead of providing another lengthy list of inspiration.

~

HOW TO USE THIS BOOK

The first half of the book discusses the common themes among those portfolios. You can use it as a reference guide to bridge any gaps in your portfolio or as a refresher to highlight areas you may have overlooked.

The second half of the book provides a list of portfolios with detailed specifications and visuals. You can directly use them as references.

For your convenience, I have compiled all the portfolio links from this book into a single database named *Top 50 Product Design Portfolios Curated from Hundreds*. As a bonus, it also includes other great portfolios that were not featured in the book.

Go to **xinranma.gumroad.com** and use the coupon code **BOOK** in the checkout to grab it for free.

Ready? Let's dive in.

PART 1

SECRETS

1

THE QUALITY OF THE UI IS PARAMOUNT

The high-fidelity user interface designs arguably matter more than anything else in your portfolio. A simple site with high-quality UI is far more competitive than a fancy-looking site with mediocre UI.

Hiring managers with keen eyes can cut to the chase and gauge a designer's capabilities by glancing at the final design. As the old saying goes, "A picture is worth a thousand words."

I understand it's challenging for some people to grasp the critical importance of UI, since product design isn't just about UI.

However, when hiring managers scan portfolios, they inevitably judge your design skills based on what they see at face value. This is especially true when they are evaluating junior or mid-level product designers.

In today's competitive job market, the quality of the UI alone can set you ahead of many candidates. Granted, it won't reveal the full spectrum of a designer's capabilities, but it can make a strong initial impression. If they are intrigued to learn more, they can follow up with an initial phone call or interview.

A common issue in many portfolios is that the final design quality isn't high enough.

But what does "high quality" even mean?

Below is a general definition of high-quality UI, although different designers may have different standards.

A high-quality UI looks familiar.

Jakob's Law, a principle established by usability expert Jakob Nielsen, states that people prefer designs that feel familiar, especially in the world of product design.

A familiar interface design aligns with what users are accustomed to. In product design, there are universal design principles and common design patterns; that's why many websites or apps of the same type utilize similar designs. Often, there's no need to reinvent the wheel.

A common issue in many aspiring designers' portfolios is that the user interface designs don't appear familiar:

- The text is smaller than the standard.
- The typography hierarchy is off.
- The styles of the CTA buttons are uncommon.

All those small details like those above can contribute to a sense of unfamiliarity.

This principle of familiarity also applies to the perceptions of hiring managers. If the UI you've designed aligns with common design patterns in their minds, you can gain their trust. Conversely, if your UI design looks uniquely different, it may raise doubts and concerns, potentially hindering your chances of receiving an interview invitation.

A high-quality UI is consistent.

When all your UI elements, such as fonts, colors, images, and icons, are consistent across screens, they create harmony and clarity.

Small inconsistencies can immediately stand out to the keen eyes of experienced designers.

Here are some examples of inconsistencies:

- The header is slightly different on each screen.
- The CTA button has many different styles.
- Some text is center-aligned, while other text is left-aligned.
- Different design components are used to address the same user behavior.

These minor details can accumulate, becoming significant distractions and potentially raising red flags.

A high-quality UI is simple.

A simple UI should avoid unnecessary elements and focus solely on what's essential. When a user interface becomes overwhelming, it confuses users and alerts hiring managers.

Resist the temptation to overload your design with excessive elements, such as unnecessary flows, too much text, and too many CTAs. Simplify information when it becomes complex and establish a clear hierarchy.

A high-quality UI is accessible.

Another common issue in many aspiring designers' portfolios is accessibility. If best practices are not followed, the UI becomes difficult to read, which can be another immediate red flag.

Three areas require extra attention:

1) Font size for body text

The font size for body text in UI design is typically no smaller than 16 pixels. It ensures readability across various devices and screen sizes.

2) Color of the body text

The body text color should provide sufficient contrast against the background color to ensure readability. I have often noticed that the gray body text in many UI designs is too light. It becomes even worse if the gray text is placed on a colored background.

3) Color contrast for CTA buttons

The CTA button is a critical design element that receives a lot of attention. The text on the button should contrast sharply with the button's background color. A contrast ratio of at least 4.5:1 for small text and 3:1 for large text is recommended. Choose a prominent button color that contrasts well with the background while still aligning with the overall design theme.

A high-quality UI has high resolution.

Use high-resolution images. It's one of the simplest things you can do to enhance the "high quality" appearance of your design.

It's unfortunate if the design is excellent but the image resolution is low. It's like you created a beautiful artwork at home but only showed others a blurry photo of it.

This issue sometimes arises from the export settings in design software or the web builder's compression after uploading. Regardless of the reason, it's crucial to pay attention to this detail.

2

PEOPLE RARELY READ

Two years ago, my team was hiring, and we received over a hundred applications within a few days after the job was posted on LinkedIn.

Imagine how many portfolios the hiring managers had to review and how much time they could spend on each one. Probably just a few minutes at most. They likely didn't have time to read every word; instead, they scanned.

Polish the homepage, particularly the top section.

So, the top section of your homepage receives extra attention. It's important to leave a strong impression when people first land on your homepage. Spending time polishing visual details to make it look very polished is worthwhile. As the saying goes, "You only get one chance to make a first impression."

The top section of Seán Halpin's homepage

Lead the case study page with a glimpse of compelling design.

Just like the homepage, it is crucial to showcase a strong visual when people first land on a case study page.

This could be an elegant mockup featuring multiple final design screens or a banner with one or two screens. The goal is to offer a sneak peek of the design result to generate excitement and encourage people to continue scrolling. Avoid starting with a wall of text at the top of the page.

What if you don't have a compelling final design to showcase?

In that case, there's a significant separate issue at hand: you need to improve your final designs. Often, you may not even be aware of this need.

9

When in doubt, seek feedback from designers with great visual craft. They can help you identify the areas that need improvement. Note that we are not even discussing user needs yet; this is merely an initial review of your UI design at face value.

Another tip is to study good real-world examples. If your design is an app, pull up a similar popular app on your phone, observe the key design details, and compare your design with it. You can also find similar examples on websites like Mobbin and Landingfolio.

Improve the text-image balance.

This is often an overlooked aspect, but it is one of the secrets behind effective portfolios.

Achieving a good balance between visuals and text significantly enhances the page's appearance. As mentioned earlier, the design visuals in your portfolio are more important than the text; you don't want people to scroll excessively before they discover them.

If there is an imbalance, it is usually due to one of two reasons: 1) Too much text or 2) Insufficient visuals in between.

When you encounter a section with too much text, aim to reduce the amount of text first. You can likely eliminate at least half of it. After all, most people don't "read" portfolios; they scan them. For the second, third, and fourth case studies in your portfolio, you can afford to cut even more text.

Reducing text is just the first step. Then, aim to alternate text and visuals on the screen in a balanced manner, rather than clustering all the text together. If you examine the examples in the second half of the book, you'll notice that almost all of them achieve a good balance by alternating text and images.

ILLUSTRATIONS

In addition to the visual language of the interface, I took inspiration from IKEA's simple illustration instructions and decided to not only instruct but also show our users what to do.

At first, I aimed to create the illustrations myself but quickly realized that given the time to launch and the amount of work still ahead, it was best that the illustrations be contracted. I contacted and interviewed illustrators and ultimately worked with an illustrator I'd come across on Dribbble, Nick Slater. I communicated the vision by giving Nick context into our goals and sending him sketches and photographs of what I had in mind. In the end, Nick created, 6 illustrations in total and I utilized the elements he provided to create additional illustrations later in the process.

MOTION DESIGN

No matter how seamless we wanted to make setup, it still had it's technical constraints. For example, it takes time for the eeros to start up before the app can connect to them and time for the modem and eero to connect to the internet. Because of this, we needed some way to show progress in the app.

After storyboarding and talking through concepts with stakeholders, I built the animations in After Effects while staying in constant communication with our mobile engineers to ensure that we were creating animations that they could build in time.

The text-image balance of Jess Chen's portfolio

An additional tip is to group text into paragraphs of comparable sizes. This strategy can prevent some paragraphs from being significantly longer than others.

3

SHOW LARGE IMAGES
IF YOU CAN

If you have compelling designs, show them prominently. You should be confident enough to showcase your design in large images, exposing every detail to the viewer's eyes.

This doesn't mean that all images should be large; only highlight the ones you are most proud of.

Consider this a pressure test:

Can you select several final design screens that you're most proud of and display them as large as possible on a case study page?

If you're not confident about those screens or if you notice some weak spots, it's time to revise them or decide not to display them at all.

If you're unsure, as mentioned in the previous chapter, it's time to seek feedback and focus on the most crucial screens you need to showcase. It's even better if those screens directly address the problem statement you've laid out in your portfolio.

Later in the book, you'll see examples where large-size final designs are common, with some spanning the entire page width.

Large image from Aris Acoba's portfolio

4

THE DEVIL IS IN THE
TYPOGRAPHIC DETAILS

Aside from visuals, typography plays a crucial role in portfolios as well. It's an often overlooked but significant indicator of a designer's capabilities.

High-caliber hiring managers can immediately discern the difference between a novice and an experienced designer by observing how they handle typography.

Moreover, the purpose of typography in portfolios isn't just to make the text look attractive. It's also about minimizing distractions to enhance the final design.

The text on a page should not distract viewers from your designs; instead, it should enhance the viewing experience. Poor or mediocre text treatment is noticeable.

Typography involves more than just choosing fonts. It also encompasses other aspects, such as hierarchy and readability.

Establish a good hierarchy.

Hierarchy is crucial. It's the first thing people notice before delving into other details.

When you scan any portfolio page, the visual hierarchy of the text stands out before the content itself. Consider a resume, which is essentially a large block of text. A glance at a resume page quickly conveys the overall appearance of the text, leaving a lasting first impression. A clear hierarchy creates harmony.

Among various typographic hierarchies, the distinction between the subheadings and body text is particularly important.

Since they are usually positioned close to each other, achieving a delicate balance can significantly impact the overall visual appearance. Some contrast is necessary to differentiate them, but too much contrast can disrupt the harmony.

In the examples from this book, it's common for the font size of the subheading to be twice as large as the body text and to make it bold. This approach, where both font size and weight contribute to establishing hierarchy, is a good rule of thumb.

The outcome

On the design side we broke components down into verified and unverified states
which signified items with code parity and those that were to be considered
experimental or work-in-progress. Components were also broken into individual
libraries that represented unique codebases — all of which pulled brand elements from
a central "Core' library.

The subheading font vs. body font from Buzz Usborne's portfolio

A common mistake regarding typographic hierarchy is the overuse of font styles within the body text. For instance, if too many words are emphasized with a bold font, then no words truly stand out. Worse yet, the entire paragraph becomes chaotic and distracting. Remember, the text should help enhance the visuals on the page rather than detract from them.

Select the right fonts.

Font selection can be a daunting task, given the endless options available.

I recommend opting for a versatile font that includes multiple weights, such as light, regular, medium, semi-bold, bold, and italic versions of each. This approach makes it easier to establish a visual hierarchy.

For the body text, the goal should be achieving the overall harmony rather than making the text itself overly distinctive. Choose fonts that are widely used by reputable designers. These are likely to be versatile and adaptive, so you don't have to reinvent the wheel.

For headlines, there is more room for creativity. You can either use a heavier weight of the same font or select a more distinctive font.

Inspire from great portfolios.

You can also draw inspiration from portfolios you admire to discover which fonts they use.

In the second half of this book, I've included a detailed typographic analysis of many sample portfolios, so you don't have to invest a lot of time figuring them out on your own.

Most of the portfolios featured in the book use only one font family. Some use popular fonts like Roboto, Helvetica, and Open Sans, while others use less familiar fonts, such as Euclid Circular A.

However, nearly all the fonts used offer a variety of weights, which makes it versatile to establish an effective hierarchy.

Examples of popular versatile fonts:

- Inter
- Lato
- Lora

- Source Sans
- Public Sans
- Work Sans
- Open Sans
- IBM Plex Serif
- Satoshi
- Manrope
- Roboto
- Nunito
- Montserrat
- Helvetica (overly popular)
- Futura (overly popular)

Some portfolios use two font families. It's not uncommon to pair two fonts—a sans-serif font for headers and a serif font for body text. This classic pairing rule establishes clear contrast while maintaining harmony between the two.

For font pairings, I suggest starting with a popular pair and then experimenting from there, such as:

(Headline + Body Text)

- Lora + Roboto
- Libre Baskerville + Source Sans
- Raleway + Source Sans
- Playfair Display + Source Sans
- Merriweather + Lato
- Prata + Lato
- Roboto + Cabin Regular
- Oswald + Cardo

- Oswald + Lora
- Any elegant serif font + Inter
- Roboto Slab + Roboto (same family; natural match)
- Source Serif + Source Sans (same family; natural match)
- Merriweather + Merriweather Sans (same family; natural match)

It's worth mentioning that a couple of portfolios in this book use a highly decorative font on the homepage to add some personality and capture attention. This is also an option, but try not to overdo it.

Make it readable.

Line length and line height significantly affect readability.

Line length refers to the width of a block of text, while line height is the vertical distance between two lines of text (measured from the baseline of one line to the baseline of the next).

In the portfolio examples featured in this book, most line lengths for text fall between 50 and 90 characters. This range is a good rule of thumb for web design, as a long line of text is difficult to read and visually unappealing.

A practical tip is to limit the maximum width of the entire page or just the text block section.

Contributing to IBM.org
Extending the CSR design system

IBM.org is a digital platform that aligns all of IBM's Corporate
Social Responsibility initiatives under a unified experience. In
order to convey the scale of the program's social impact,
IBM.org's design system is more editorial inspired than IBM's
core brand. My main responsibility was to find opportunities to
extend this brand expression into each initiative's design
system in order to maintain brand alignment and consistency.

Single-column layout for text from Michael Lo's portfolio

It is also common to convert text into two columns—one
for section headings and one for section body text. This
automatically reduces the width of the text block to a
desirable value.

Improving the referral dashboard

Business need   ReferralCandy was starting to lag behind newer competitors and
needed to become a more modern piece of software, show more useful
analytics, and improve its performance to become more useful to
merchants.

Goal   Update the dashboard to show more relevant analytics, add new
capabilities to increase product-led growth. The bottomline was to have
more merchants paying for the product tracked by monthly recurring
revenue (MRR).

Personal challenge   ReferralCandy is a 10+ year old product. The many years brought with it
performance issues, and an outdated platform. Making any changes,
even seemingly simple ones meant trying to untangle many years of
legacy code.

This project was a 7-month long project broken up into sizable chunks
where I defined the strategy with key stakeholders and collaborated
with engineering on various technical challenges, while keeping the
design team motivated and inspired.

Two-column layout for text from Ben George's portfolio

Another common practice to improve readability is to vary the background color for different sections. This helps divide a long page into digestible chunks.

Sections with different background colors from Yuha Kim's portfolio

5

NOT ALL CASE STUDIES RECEIVE THE SAME LEVEL OF ATTENTION

If you only have less than a minute to review someone's portfolio, how would you navigate?

You would likely visit the homepage, probably view the first case study page, and possibly browse the second case study page. But what about the third or fourth case study? Most people don't even get to read them.

So it's crucial to ensure that the first case study shown on the homepage demonstrates your best work.

Likewise, you need to invest more time and effort in your first case study than in the others. I often recommend designers prioritize that case study. Once that case study reaches a good stage, it's much easier to replicate the same structure for the second case study and make adjustments from there.

As for the third, fourth, and fifth case studies (you may not even need to have that many), you can allocate less energy and keep them simple. You may only highlight the special features and not include much else.

There is a concept called The Bucket Effect. Imagine you have a bucket made out of boards of different heights. The amount of water the bucket can hold isn't determined by the tallest board, but by the shortest one, because water will spill out from the lowest point.

Similarly, when it comes to a designer's portfolio, it is only as strong as your weakest piece. So for the case studies that people have limited time to scan, keep them simple and only showcase the best. Less is more.

6

THE DESIGN EXPLORATION IS MORE EFFECTIVE THAN THE DESIGN PROCESS

The design process included in your portfolio carries much less weight than your final design. Many people have stressed this. Almost ten years ago, it was common to see a lot of design processes in a UX portfolio as the gold standard; however, this practice has shifted over recent years as the job market has become increasingly saturated and competition intensified.

Everyone has a design process, but not everyone can end up with great designs. The final design showcased in your portfolio has become even more important for you to stand out from hundreds of portfolios. If hiring managers and recruiters are interested in you and want to learn more about the reasoning behind your designs, they will contact you and invite you to interviews where you can articulate your designs in depth.

As the effectiveness of displaying the design process in the portfolio diminishes, what is worth including besides the final design? The answer is design exploration.

What is design exploration?

Design exploration is technically part of your design process. In the context of this book, it specifically refers to the high-fidelity design options that you created during the design process.

You might recall the low-fidelity designs you explored. I don't recommend including those as much—at least keep them to a minimum in your portfolio. The rationale behind this is that in the day-to-day job of a product designer, there are numerous design explorations at the high-fidelity level. High-fidelity design explorations not only demonstrate your ability to think divergently with compelling designs but also showcase your high level of craftsmanship.

If you are a career changer, I understand that this can be a significant challenge and dilemma. You probably have limited time and space to explore design options at a high-fidelity level.

This is especially the case for bootcamp projects. Due to the bootcamp curriculum, the time allocated for developing your design was insufficient. It's common for students to proceed with one design idea early on and develop it all the way to the final high-fidelity designs within a couple of weeks. How can the depth of those designs be compared to those developed over months?

If you face the same challenge of not having compelling design options to show, it's time to work on them.

How to develop high-fidelity design options when you don't have any.

Before you begin, you need to ask yourself a question:

Is this the case study you want to rank first on the home-page of your portfolio?

If the answer is no, then you may not need to spend the effort to dig deeper.

If the answer is yes, then it is worth the effort. Next, look at the final design of the project and ask yourself the following questions:

- Did the design solve the customer/business problems you stated?
- How effective was the design?
- What was the major design decision you made before settling on this final design?
- Were there other design options that you didn't get a chance to explore but could have solved those problems well?

Think about the answers to these questions.

Then, look at your final design and imagine if there was a "crossroads moment" before you settled on it. It refers to a moment later in your design process when you had two or three design options that were all compelling. Each had its pros and cons. You considered the trade-offs and made an important design decision to proceed with one of those options, which became your final design.

If you can identify that "crossroads" moment and develop the design options into two or three high-fidelity design options, you will complete the heavy lifting of the design exploration. You can then supplement it with necessary text or callouts to articulate your design decision.

You may wonder why I am introducing this "crossroads" idea. I propose to craft the most important highlight of your design exploration first.

Starting with identifying two or three compelling design options at a critical moment of your design exploration is much more effective than spending a month exploring numerous ideas without focus. And it sounds less intimidating too. As the 80-20 rule states, 80% of outcomes result from 20% of inputs. Start with crafting the most exciting highlight of your case study if you don't have it yet.

In summary, these design exploration highlights not only make your portfolio look more sophisticated but also can significantly help you in future interviews when you need to present your work and articulate your design explorations, which is ultimately a bigger challenge than the portfolio itself. You're killing two birds with one stone.

You may still wonder: "But the project is already completed... How can I go back and develop those ideas further?"

Yes, it's acceptable to further develop the project even after it is "completed". This shouldn't prevent you from continuing to work on the areas where you didn't have the time and resources previously.

Ultimately, interviewers care less about the reasons you didn't push your design further; they more care about what you are capable of designing.

7

KEEP THE NAVIGATION SIMPLE
AND EFFECTIVE

The baseline of a product design portfolio is its usability. While you focus on the visual design and content, don't lose sight of usability.

All the portfolios in this book are relatively easy to navigate. The basic principles of Interaction Design also apply to portfolios.

Here is a checklist from my first book *The Minimalist Career Changer*:

- The website is fast to load.
- Your resume is easy to find.
- Your case studies are easy to find.
- Your contact information is easy to find.
- All the links are working.
- The navigation is intuitive on mobile devices.
- It is easy to return to the homepage after landing on a page.

- It is easy to go to the next case study after viewing one.

If you look at the examples in this book, although each of them has a distinct personality, the navigation is simple and effective.

8

ADD SOME PERSONALITY

In the competitive job market today, an authentic personal brand is more important than ever before. It's impressive to see the level of creative detail in those portfolios, adding a personal touch.

Broken grid layout

The easiest and safest way for web layout is to make alignments and follow the grid. However, a well-designed broken grid layout creates a unique experience. It's about adding a little asymmetry or overlap to make the website attractive. It's not easy, but if you can pull it off, your portfolio can stand out.

Shopify Pay is the first buyer-facing product Shopify created to simplify and streamline the tedious parts of shopping to let people focus on the parts that they love.

In practice, Shopify Pay allows buyers to opt in to save their information at checkout and be able to automatically reuse it on any other Shopify store. While the core concept is fairly simple to grasp, we thought it would be helpful to provide a page for people to get all of the information on how it works.

Our Goals

1 To show people how simple the experience is and set the right expectation for what will happen at their next purchase.

2 Reassure people of the trustworthiness of Shopify as the guardian of people's information. After all for many people, this is the first time they heard of Shopify. It was really important for us to give an explanation of who we are and what we do.

3 The last goal was to give people a place to opt-out that was front and center. We didn't want to bury it or hide it. If you've signed up by mistake or change your mind, it should be as easy to opt-out as it was to opt-in.

A big question we had was "should we include the standard Shopify navigation?" While we all liked the consistency of including the same navigation as the rest of the website we ultimately decided to not include it. Why? Because the audience of this website are buyers, not merchants. Including things like our pricing page in the navigation here would've added more confusion than clarity. It's a great example of how consistency is a not a goal in and of itself. In this case, consistency was working against our goal of creating a simple and clear message for our intended audience.

In this case, consistency was working against our goal of creating a simple and clear message for our intended audience.

A broken grid layout from Kevin Clark's portfolio

The Section of Writing

It is delightful to see samples of writing included on some portfolio websites. Some are about perspectives on product design, while others delve into personal life or hobbies. Articles and blog posts are great ways to showcase a designer's viewpoints. It is one of the effective ways to demonstrate your depth of thinking and authentic personality.

Articles

Homemade Pizza Cheat Sheet
I'd like to preface this article by saying I'm by no means an expert on making your own pizza. I just recently started dabbling in making my own dough...

Read more →

2019 Gift Guide
I'm a notoriously difficult person to buy gifts for. With this holiday season coming up, I thought I'd take a stab at curating a list of gift ideas...

Read more →

Clockwise 322
I was privileged enough to be a guest on Clockwise this week. We talked about the California DMV selling your personal data, the video recording and...

Read more →

Shopify Email
I'm so happy to finally be able to share with the world Shopify Email. It's an email marketing tool built from the ground up for commerce. Even if...

Read more →

Writing samples from Kevin Clark's portfolio

Logo

Almost all the portfolios include elegant, well-crafted logos. It is the little detail that people will notice when they first land on your portfolio website.

Logo from Buzz Usborne's portfolio

Copy

Some portfolios have personalized copy that connects with the audience.

TALKING POINTS

I write in all caps. Pilot G-Tec pens rock. Baking helps to calm me. Once upon a time, I wanted to be a vet. I love old people. Messiest desk in the office, most organized Sketch files in the ~~land~~ bay.

Copy from Jess Chen's portfolio

Favicon

Favicon is the tiny icon used on web browsers to represent a website. It can help increase visibility and strengthen your brand's identity. Every web builder has its default favicon, but you can always upload your own. It can add some personality.

Favicon from Chengsu Chen's portfolio

PART 2

EXAMPLES

9

DISCLAIMER

Before going through all the portfolio examples, there are some disclaimer items I would like to address.

1. There is no singular definition of great portfolios.

You'll see that some portfolios I included have minimalist designs, while others are incredibly thorough with details. Some portfolios highlight themselves as thought leaders, while others let the elegant designs speak for themselves.

Every portfolio is different. Different designers have different strengths and want to brand themselves differently. Yes, there are some common themes, but there are no right or wrong answers when it comes to portfolios.

2. This is not an exhaustive list.

Everyone has different preferences for portfolios. I'm sure there are other great portfolios that I am not aware of or could have included in this book but didn't.

If you discover a great portfolio like that, I would greatly appreciate it if you could send me a message on **xinran-ma.com**. I will consider adding it to the portfolio database that I mentioned in the Introduction so other people can benefit from it too.

3. Some are updated frequently; some are not.

Some portfolios are being updated frequently. So don't be surprised if the portfolio looks different from the time I wrote this, or maybe the whole site has expired! This is just the fluid nature of portfolios.

Some portfolios, however, have not been updated for years. A few of them even have projects that date back to 2017 or 2018. I still included them because they stand the test of time. On the other hand, I also made sure not to include ones that are no longer relevant.

4. The specifications are based on Desktop.

You will notice I included detailed font specifications for every portfolio. Note that the font size and line height are based on Desktop. For Mobile, you may need to scale the font size and line height slightly for readability.

As a rule of thumb, the font size and line height of the body text are almost the same across Mobile and Desktop, while the font size and line height of the headings are smaller on Mobile. It may sound complicated, but if you're using a website builder, the built-in responsive capabilities should take care of this.

5. The examples are not ranked.

There is no ranking of the examples that I will show. They follow a random order. The portfolios I show earlier on the list are no better than the ones I show later.

10

YUHA KIM'S PORTFOLIO

Website URL: https://yuha.work/

Website Builder: Squarespace

Keyword
- Minimalist
- Elegant

Color
- #FFFFFF
- #F7F7F7
- #C62828
- #191B1F

Main Heading Font
- Font Family: Spectral
- Font Weight: Light
- Font Size: 2 rem

- Line Height: 1.3 rem

Body Text Font
- Font Family: Helvetica Neue
- Font Weight: Regular
- Font Size: 1 rem
- Line Height: 1.7 rem

～

HOMEPAGE

Top Navigation Bar
- UX/UI
- Fashion
- About

Structure
- Short Bio
- Case Study 1
- Case Study 2
- Case Study 3
- Case Study 4
- Case Study 5
- Vision Projects

Visuals
- Full-width case study thumbnails that span the entire page.
- High-quality UI displayed in the thumbnails.

- Elegant fonts with effective pairings.

∼

CASE STUDY PAGE

Structure
- Project Overview
  - *Context*
  - *My roles*
  - *Impact*
- Understanding
  - *The user*
  - *The task*
  - *The tool*
- Project Goal & Scope
- Project Task I
  - *Problems*
  - *Approach*
  - *Design Decision*
- Project Task II
  - *Problems*
  - *Approach*
  - *Design Decision*
  - *Implementation & Feedback*
- Project Task III
  - *Problems*
  - *Approach*
  - *Design Decision*
  - *Wireframe*

- *Output*
- Design System
  - *Impact*
  - *Reflection*

Visuals
- Sections with different background colors.
- Subheadings in bold red font.
- Two-column layout with the body text in one column.
- Strong visual hierarchy between the serif heading font and the sans-serif body font.

∾

SPECIAL SAUCE

- A delicate GIF on the About page showcases the progression of her design career.
- Diverse works reflect her experience as a former creative director.
- The portfolio consistently demonstrates strong visual craftsmanship.

Meet Yuha! A Creative-Problem Solving Designer based in SF.
Yuha specializes in transforming complex concepts into
Simple and visually appealing narratives.

CertiK | Core Internal Tool Redesign

Homepage from Yuha Kim's Portfolio

Keep the team's work **flowing**
and increase **efficiency** while making
the tool **scalable** and **user-friendly**

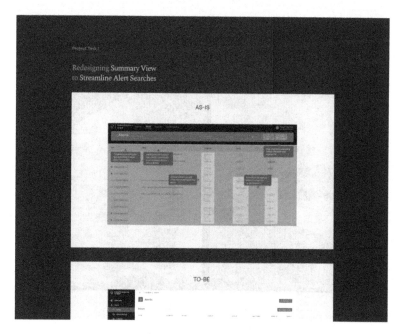

Case Study Page from Yuha Kim's Portfolio

Yuha embraces ambiguity and thrives in unfamiliar territory.
With her exposed to new tasks, ideas flow effortlessly within minutes.
Anywhere she goes, it feels like her nest.

About Page from Yuha Kim's Portfolio

Career Pivot by Yuha Kim / acrylic painting

About Page from Yuha Kim's Portfolio

11

OISHEE SEN'S PORTFOLIO

Website URL: https://www.oishee.io/

Website Builder: Squarespace

Keyword
- Personal
- Whimsical
- Delightful

Color
- #FFFFFF
- #F8F6F4
- #000000

Main Heading Font
- Font Family: General Sans
- Font weight: Semi-bold
- Font Size: 2 rem

- Line Height: 1.23

Body Text Font
- Font Family: General Sans
- Font weight: Regular
- Font Size: 1 rem
- Line Height: 1.43

HOMEPAGE

Top Navigation Bar
- Work
- Love
- About
- Resume

Structure
- Bio (Keywords)
- Case Study 1
- Case Study 2
- Case Study 3
- Case Study 4
- Case Study 5
- Features
- Archived Projects (2016-2018)
- What I Love
- About Me

Visuals

• Large, prominent headings accompanied by attractive icons.

• Well-designed, delightful thumbnails.

CASE STUDY PAGE

Structure

• Project Overview
  - *My Role*
  - *The Team*
  - *Timeline*
• Final Design Walkthrough
• Focus Area Overview
• Focus Area 1
  - *Problem Statement*
  - *Design Decisions*
  - *Validate with Users*
• Focus Area 2
  - *Problem Statement*
  - *Design Decisions*
• Focus Area 3
  - *Problem Statement*
  - *Design Decisions*
• Focus Area 4
  - *Problem Statement*
  - *Design Decisions*

Visuals

• Subheadings in all caps to establish a visual hierarchy with the body text.

• Three columns displaying "My Role", "The Team", and "Timeline", are commonly used in other portfolios as well.

~

SPECIAL SAUCE

- A cohesive visual language is applied throughout the portfolio website.
- Both the "Love" page and the "About" page exhibit a strong personal brand.
- Media Mentions are included in the "Features" section, highlighting her achievements.

Curious designer, image maker, storyteller

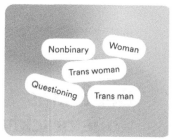

Making Bumble inclusive for every gender
Product Design / 2021

Bringing the power of videos to Bumble
Product Design / 2021

Homepage from Oishee Sen's Portfolio

53

Outlook on the Mobile Web

INTRODUCTION

Early 2020, we shipped a brand new experience for Microsoft Outlook on the mobile web which is now used by over 65 million people a month. This involved a revamp of the inbox, calendar, people and search experiences while addressing the unique nuances of designing for PWAs and mobile web.

MY ROLE	THE TEAM	TIMELINE
Responsible for research, concept ideation, design, user testing and delivery of key concepts and feature areas	4 designers, 3 product managers and 11+ engineers	March 2019 - Jan 2020

Case Study Page from Oishee Sen's Portfolio

Extra! Extra!

In Japanese, my name 'Oishee' means **delicious!**

I've had a **fringe** almost all my life, which also means that very few people have actually seen my forehead.

I love games with strong characters, fictional worlds and incredible storylines.

✦ I'm currently playing **God of War: Ragnarok**

This article about AI by Tim Urban from his blog **Wait But Why** got me really interested in technology and digital futures.

About Page from Oishee Sen's Portfolio

STORYTELLING

I love storytelling for product and people

I thoroughly enjoy experimenting with video making, motion design, filmmaking, video editing and presentations to communicate stories of product and people.

Love Page from Oishee Sen's Portfolio

12

JENNIFER WONG'S PORTFOLIO

Website URL: https://www.jenniferywong.com/

Website Builder: Webflow

Keyword:
- Comprehensive
- Detailed
- Professional

Color:
- #FFFFFF
- #27282E

Main Heading Font:
- Font Family: Circular Std
- Font Weight: Black
- Font Size: 1.67 rem
- Line Height: 1.4

Body Text Font:
- Font Family: Avenir Next
- Font Weight: Regular
- Font Size: 1 rem
- Line Height: 1.7

HOMEPAGE

Top Navigation Bar
- Home
- About
- Resume
- Writing

Structure
- Bio
- Case Study 1
- Case Study 2
- Case Study 3
- Case Study 4
- Case Study 5
- Case Study 6
- Case Study 7
- Case Study 8
- Case Study 9
- Case Study 10

Visuals

• Project thumbnails with a coherent visual style.

• Project thumbnails with project overviews, types, and success metrics.

~

CASE STUDY PAGE

Structure

• Project Overview
  - *Role*
  - *Timeline*
  - *Core Responsibilities*
• Problem & Insights
• Solution
• Result with Success Metrics
• Additional Context
  - *Feature 1 (Before & After)*
  - *Feature 2 (Before & After)*
  - *Feature 3 (Before & After)*
  - *Feature 4 (Before & After)*
• Soft Launch - Feedback Gathering
• Future Steps
• Reflection

Visuals

• A large amount of text, yet balanced with a large amount of images.

• Left navigation panel featuring section names to improve reading experience.

SPECIAL SAUCE

• The "About Me" page showcases her design values, personality, and hobbies.
• Multiple areas emphasize the impact of the designs, highlighting her professional experience.

I'm a strategic and AI-driven Product Designer (ex Dropbox)

Armed with a Master's in Design from UC Berkeley, I was recently a Staff Product Designer at Poised (AI communication coach). I specialize in product strategy, systems thinking, design craft, leadership, and team collaboration. My journey spans entrepreneurship to enterprise, always innovating and pushing boundaries. On a lighter note, I'm a proud cat whisperer AND dog lover!

(AI/ML) (B2B) (B2C) (Mobile) (Web) (Design Systems) (Branding)

AI/ML / B2C / Desktop

Poised - Inspiring Clear & Confident Online Communication for Professionals and Job Interviewees

As the design lead at Poised, an AI communication coach for online meetings, I played a pivotal strategic role, driving initiatives that more than doubled user retention and increased free trial conversion rates by 40+%.

B2B / B2C / Web

Dropbox - Streamlining Access To Shared Cloud Storage for Non-Dropbox users

I proactively identified friction in the signup journey for non-Dropbox users, proposed redesigning it, and helped prioritize it on the product roadmap. Released in Sep '21.

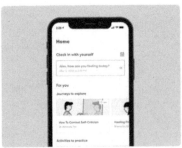

AI/ML / B2C / Mobile

Empathie - Cultivating Inclusive & Accessible Mental Wellness For Asian Americans

Empathie, a company I co-founded, is a self-guided mobile app for early

B2B / Web

Procore - Creating Flexibility For Fund Transfers

Procore is the world's #1 most-used construction management software. I was the first to redesign the 2-year, #1 customer-requested feature for

Homepage from Jennifer Wong's Portfolio

60

Providing AI-driven, personalized and actionable guidance for clearer communication in online meetings

As I directed the product and content designers, our collective efforts pivoted Poised from a passive homepage to a dynamically active, user-centric interface, intertwining continuous personalized suggestions with substantive feedback. My strategic emphasis shifted from a purely metrics-focused approach to one that harmoniously melded immediate feedback with anticipatory tips and a balance of qualitative and quantitative insights, thereby notably enhancing user engagement and efficaciously enabling them to refine their communication skills.

Shifting from Poised being passive to action-oriented

Homepage + site architecture

Before

Passive and something fragmented

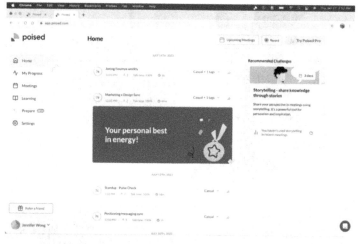

After

Ability to review past meetings right away, see relevant suggestions on how to improve, and prepare with ease

Case Study Page from Jennifer Wong's Portfolio

Family

My partner and I are proud cat parents living in Williamsburg, Brooklyn

Say hello to Suki (Akatsuki) and Roara (Incineroar)! Suki (left), our vocal 'golden-retriever' cat, steals food and is quite the trickster - from sitting to spinning! Roara (right) is our athletic nurturer. She might be shy, but she's our chief cuddler, always there during our lows. As for my partner, he's a full-time entrepreneur with a college admissions consultancy. Our worlds collided through my startup venture; after a speaking event, his friend introduced us, leading to an unforgettable concert night.

Visit our cats' insta

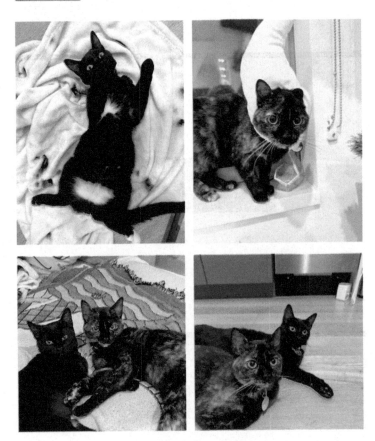

About Page from Jennifer Wong's Portfolio

13

KEVIN CLARK'S PORTFOLIO

Website URL: https://kevinclark.ca/

Website Builder: Gatsby

Keyword
- Thoughtful
- Engaging
- Modern

Color
- #FFFFFF
- #F1F1F1

Main Heading Font
- Font Family: Graphik
- Font Weight: Medium
- Font Size: 2 rem
- Line Height: 1.3

Body Text Font
- Font Family: Graphik
- Font Weight: Regular
- Font Size: 1 rem
- Line Height: 1.7

~

HOMEPAGE

Top Navigation Bar
- Articles
- Work
- Speaking
- About

Structure
- Bio (Keywords)
- Case Study 1
- Case Study 2
- Case Study 3
- Latest Articles

Visuals
- Broken grid layouts.
- Overlapping elements (Text & Card; Text & Text).
- Friendly self-portrait.

CASE STUDY PAGE

Structure
- Project Context
- User Journey
- User Research
- The Plan
- Setback
- Design Explorations
- Final Design
- What I Learned

Visuals
- Unconventional, descriptive headlines.
- Broken grid layouts featuring large text to create a more dynamic rhythm.

~

SPECIAL SAUCE

- The storytelling is authentic and vivid rather than following strict templates.
- A creative and well-balanced layout is applied throughout the portfolio.
- The "Articles" page showcases his thoughtful personality and great taste in design.
- The "Speaking" page, featuring photos, social mentions,

and presentation slides, reinforces his brand as a thought leader in the field.

Homepage from Kevin Clark's Portfolio

Weather Line

Get it on the App Store →

The best weather app for iOS just got even better. Super Forecast lets you combine data from the #1 forecasting, rain, and radar services, adds a radar view and tons more.

Ryan came to me a few months ago with a really good idea of what he wanted Weather Line 2 to be. He had a solid feature set and he already had made some rough mockups of the structure of the app. All he needed was someone to solve a few UX problems and visually bring the app to life. Normally I would just say no to projects like this, but I couldn't pass up the opportunity to collaborate with Ryan.

Since we worked on the app 100% remotely, working in Figma proved invaluable. It allowed us to quickly brainstorm ideas together or asynchronously.

Case Study Page from Kevin Clark's Portfolio

Positive affect

Customers should feel positive about progress in their order status. The availability of order status information should also help eliminate confusion, friction or frustration from the online shopping process.

Trust

Customers should trust that their order status information lives in a secure location.

Orientation

Customers should be able to determine where order status information is located and arrive there efficiently.

We then started to explore different ideas for how to best present the information we wanted to present. My first idea was to treat it like a message thread. Events would show up in a linear fashion. I thought it was a clever way to see a history of your package over time.

The timeline... didn't work out

The more I worked on it, the more I realized that the full history didn't matter that much. Most people care about where their shipment is right now, not two weeks ago. It also raised a lot of questions around where should the most recent content appear, at the top or at the bottom of the page? So I decided to move on to a different concept.

Cards

Next, I thought about using collapsible cards to display only the most relevant information, but also giving a him of what came before. This direction obviously worked a lot better than the first one, but it felt like something was missing. This

Case Study Page from Kevin Clark's Portfolio

14

LIZA BEL'S PORTFOLIO

Website URL: https://creamzy.com/

Website Builder: Semplice

Keyword
- Professional
- High-quality
- Minimalist

Color
- #FFFFFF
- #F5F5F5

Main Heading Font
- Font Family: Helvetica Now
- Font Weight: Bold
- Font Size: 2 rem
- Line Height: 2.66

Body Text Font
- Font Family: Helvetica Now
- Font Weight: Regular
- Font Size: 1 rem
- Line Height: 1.66

~

HOMEPAGE

Top Navigation Bar
- Contact Me

Structure
- Short Bio
- Case Study 1
- Case Study 2
- Case Study 3
- Case Study 4
- Case Study 5

Visuals
- Well-designed high-fidelity card thumbnails.
- Clean and minimalist aesthetics.

~

CASE STUDY PAGE

Structure
- Problem
- Exploration Overview
- Exploration 1
- Exploration 2
- Exploration 3

Visuals
- Large images that span the entire page.
- High-fidelity UI demonstrating exceptional design craftsmanship.

~

SPECIAL SAUCE

- Numerous large and detailed designs.
- High-quality design explorations
- High-fidelity animated prototypes.

San Francisco based Product Designer
Former **Yelp**, **GitLab**, **Trifacta**, along with a handful of startups

Breaking down ambiguous problems into actionable and discrete projects is what I do the best.

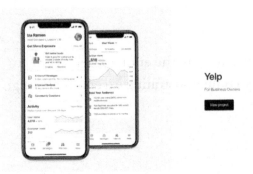

Yelp

For Business Owners

View project

GitLab

A complete DevOps platform

View project

Homepage from Liza Bel's Portfolio

What brings Yelp-merchants to the service

MTBs	Reviews	User Contributions	Customer Leads	Moderation

What creates Y4BO value as a product

Ad Campaigns	MTBs	User Contributions	Reviews	CTA button & promotions

Exploration 1

This exploration targets the minimal set of changes to make the app more engaging and easy to use but also not disrupt the user experience too much.

Case Study Page from Liza Bel's Portfolio

Final deliverables

Disclaimer: This project presents visual explorations, the detailed case study is available by request.

Milestones in GitLab are a way to track issues and merge requests created to achieve a broader goal in a certain period of time. Milestones allow you to organize issues and merge requests into a cohesive group, with an optional start date and an optional due date.

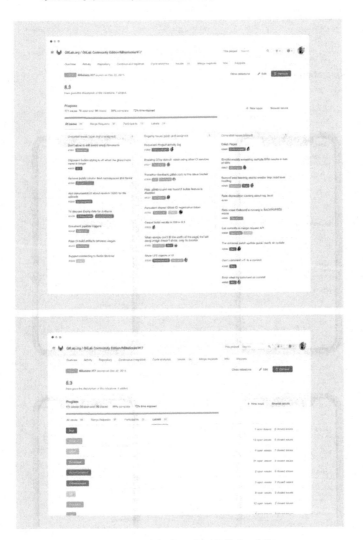

Case Study Page from Liza Bel's Portfolio

15

SASCHA EREMIN'S PORTFOLIO

Website URL: https://saschas.ai/

Website Builder: Semplice

Keyword:
- Modern
- Interactive
- Professional

Color:
- #000000
- #F01F39
- #FFFFFF
- #999999

Main Heading Font:
- Font Family: Euclid Circular A
- Font Weight: Regular

- Font Size: 1.4 rem
- Line Height: 1.43

Body Text Font:
- Font Family: Euclid Circular A
- Font Weight: Light
- Font Size: 1 rem
- Line Height: 1.6

~

HOMEPAGE

Top Navigation Bar
- Work
- About
- Contact

Structure
- Short Bio
- Case Study 1
- Case Study 2
- Case Study 3
- Case Study 4
- Case Study 5
- Case Study 6
- Say Hi

Visuals
- Black background with white text.

- Attention-grabbing red text as highlights.
- Exceptionally designed thumbnails.
- Custom cursor as a red dot.

∽

CASE STUDY PAGE

Structure
- Project Overview
- Problem
- Feature 1 Showcase
- Feature 2 Showcase
- Feature 3 Showcase
- Feature 4 Showcase
- Product Demo Video
- Learnings

Visuals
- Two-column layout with the body text in one column.
- The text blocks alternated between the left and right column.
- High-quality UI and compelling sketches.

SPECIAL SAUCE

- The red elements help create a strong visual brand through the website.
- A great visual balance between text and images is shown on every case study page.
- Text is broken into small digestible chunks.
- The website is simple with thoughtful details.

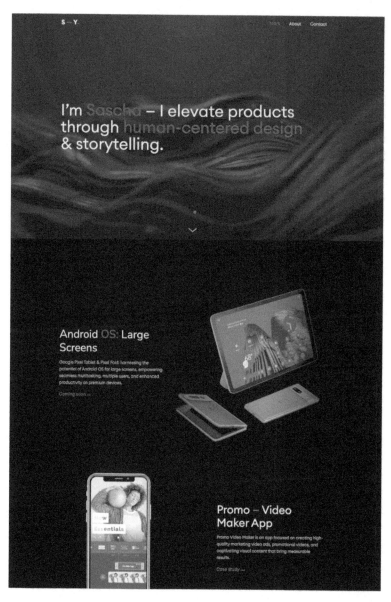

Homepage from Sascha Eremin's Portfolio

Promo Video Maker is a marketing video creation app on your mobile phone. Choose a video template, add footage and music, customize eye-catching text styles and you're ready to promote your business.

Defining the Problem

After the success of the Promo web editor and some of the insights we've got working on it, we came up with the hypothesis that making videos on tablets and phones should be fast, fun and easy so we framed our questions as how might we help our users to create video ads on their mobile devices using the real-time preview technology to simplify the user flow.

We were researching fundamental problems and oppotunities around how to transfer the web experience into mobile in an easier-to-use and elegant way emphasising the benefits of mobile platforms. I led the design of both iOS and Android apps from the ground up which is always super exciting and challenging.

Feed and Video Search

Think about what it's like to open a feed with plenty of professionally designed video templates for every national holiday, marketing event, and online trend on your phone and start editing it right away.

Well, that's already half the battle for the user struggling how to make a video for their business. I decided to show templates almost edge-to-edge and let the content shine to present people how the potential ads might look like on the phone screen.

Case Study Page from Sascha Eremin's Portfolio

I wanted to make sure the experience of adding new text to the clip is just a click of a mouse, so I focused on a simple display of the main quick controls: text position pad, clear call to actions "Add text" and "Justify text", "Select all" text styles button and a new cool feature "Shuffle style", a style randomizer. We also information hierarchy Text / Background Tabs.

Next Steps and Learnings

The released version of the editor has been well received by our customers and showed positive results. However, our team and stakeholders were already dreaming of much bigger challenges that would make the tool the leading service in its niche: video timeline and multiclips support, aspect ratio picker and animated text styles, projects I've been part of in the following iterations.

My main takeaway back then was that having a big ego does not help you work better with others, designs should be a way to help your team make wiser product decisions. As well as the time for research and test throughout the project is indisputable in the long run. It's always helpful to encourage coworkers to join the testing sessions and share the insights early on.

Case Study Page from Sascha Eremin's Portfolio

16

ARIS ACOBA'S PORTFOLIO

Website URL: https://www.arisacoba.com/

Website Builder: 11TY

Keyword:
- Interactive
- High-quality
- Sophisticated

Color:
- #F6F7F2
- #E6E6DD
- #222222
- #E1E0E6

Main Heading Font:
- Font Family: Moderat
- Font Weight: Regular

- Font Size: 2 rem
- Line Height: 1.21

Body Text Font:
- Font Family: Moderat
- Font Weight: Regular
- Font Size: 1 rem
- Line Height: 1.76

∾

HOMEPAGE

Top Navigation Bar
- Work
- About
- Contact

Structure
- Bio
- Case Study 1
- Case Study 2
- Case Study 3
- Case Study 4
- Case Study 5
- Case Study 6
- How I Work
- About Me

Visuals
- Cohesive, well-designed card thumbnails.
- Great text hierarchy above every card.
- Animated graphic elements with special effects when the cursor hovers over them.

~

CASE STUDY PAGE

Structure
- Introduction
    - *Role*
    - *Scope*
    - *Company*
    - *Location*
- Project Overview
- Feature 1 Showcase
- Feature 2 Showcase
- Feature 3 Showcase
- Feature 4 Showcase
- Dig In (Design Explorations)
- Takeaways

Visuals
- Full-width, in-depth, high-quality designs that span the entire page.
- Animated GIFs demonstrate exceptional design craftsmanship.

• Broken grid layouts create a dynamic reading experience.

~

SPECIAL SAUCE

- It is a well-crafted portfolio all around, featuring high-quality designs and refreshing interactive details.
- The Playground section on the About page showcases creative motion graphics as side projects.
- Personal, day-to-day photos add a lot of personality.

Homepage from Aris Acoba's Portfolio

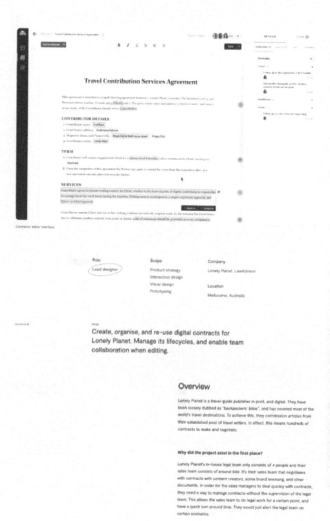

Case Study Page from Aris Acoba's Portfolio

Consultant page on unverified status   Verifying a consultant

03 Billing and Timesheets
Create, approve, or decline invoices, and manage filing of timesheets

Invoice page, and timesheet page

04 Matter management
Transition the project to a matter. Manage it from milestones to tasks,
events, and activities

Matter page

Case Study Page from Aris Acoba's Portfolio

/ah-rees ah-koh-ba/

My name is Aris Acoba ◁⋅
I've been a product, and web designer for a combination of 9 years.

I am currently working at GitHub as a product designer, helping build the tools for people who like building software.

I was previously the Head of Design at LawAdvisor.
Before the pandemic hit, I was fortunate to be sent to

About Page from Aris Acoba's Portfolio

17

BEN GEORGE'S PORTFOLIO

Website URL: https://heybengeorge.com/

Website Builder: Framer

Keyword
- Sleek
- Simple
- Professional

Color
- #FFFFFF
- #000000
- #2E5FFF

Main Heading Font
- Font Family: Mackinac Pro
- Font Weight: Book
- Font Size: 1.67 rem

- Line Height: 1.4

Body Text Font
- Font Family: System Font
- Font Weight: Regular
- Font Size: 1 rem
- Line Height: 1.5

HOMEPAGE

Top Navigation Bar
- Work
- Writing
- Speaking
- Course
- About

Structure
- Short Bio
- Case Study 1
- Case Study 2
- Case Study 3
- Case Study 4
- Case Study 5
- Recent Articles
- Side Projects
- What Colleagues Have Said

Visuals
- Animated gradient background above the fold.
- Clean, sleek card thumbnails
- Light/dark mode toggle in the top navigation bar

~

CASE STUDY PAGE

Structure
- Project Introduction
  - *Summary*
  - *Design Team*
  - *Timeline*
- Company and Team Overview
- Key Project 1
  - *Business Need*
  - *Goal*
  - *Personal Challenge*
- Results
- Key Project 2
  - *Business Need*
  - *Goal*
  - *Role*
  - *Results*
- Key Project 3
  - *Business Need*
  - *Goal*
  - *Role*
  - *Results*

- Key Project 4
  - *Business Need*
  - *Goal*
  - *Role*
  - *Results*
- Testimonial

Visuals

- Left navigation panel featuring section names to improve the reading experience.
- Divider lines between sections.
- Simple, clean visuals.

~

SPECIAL SAUCE

- All the case studies follow a simple structure.
- The Speaking and Courses pages demonstrate his thought leadership.
- The Writing page showcases his depth and width of knowledge in design.

Hi! I'm Ben George.

An experienced leader and versatile product designer living in Nürnberg, Germany.

Work

Designing for commerce

SHOPIFY
2023

Rethinking referrals for merchants

REFERRALCANDY
2021

Homepage from Ben George's Portfolio

Rethinking referrals for online merchants

As the Head of Design, I was responsible for the merchant experience on Referralcandy.com, hired and built a lean team of designers, and helped ReferralCandy grow its business revenue.

Summary

I created design hiring rubrics, interviewing strategies, and leveling frameworks for a small design department, inclusive of product design, UX research, and marketing.

Drove revenue growth by influencing product, marketing, and customer support functions as a key member of the leadership team.

Created a design system to unify components, styles, grids, typography, and iconography to improve the efficiency of design delivery.

Design team

Pham Thanh Ha, Product Designer
Desmond Chua, Researcher
Joo Tat Low, Sr. Product Designer
Bobby Kariyatty, Sr. Product Designer
Divyanshu Thakur, Product Designer
Rachel Leung, Product Designer

Timeline

2015-2018

Overview

ReferralCandy is a referral platform for online businesses through which they can scale their word of mouth marketing, drive revenue sustainably, and cultivate customer loyalty.

Case Study Page from Ben George's Portfolio

Talks

I enjoy speaking about the intersection between design and technology, building design teams, growing as a leader, creativity and many more.

One thing I love about the world of technology is that you have to be continually learning new things. A big part of my career is sharing with others my process designing experiences used by millions of people. My talks range from inspirational to more practical ones filled with real-world examples and tips that people can apply into their own work. My goal is to give people a good time while hopefully teaching them a thing or two.

Here's my speaker bio.

Speaker inquiry

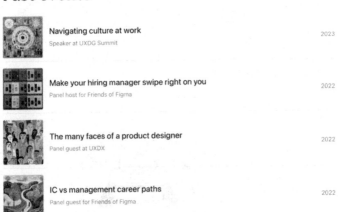

Past events

| | Navigating culture at work | 2023 |
| Speaker at UXDG Summit | |

Make your hiring manager swipe right on you — 2022
Panel host for Friends of Figma

The many faces of a product designer — 2022
Panel guest at UXDX

IC vs management career paths — 2022
Panel guest for Friends of Figma

Writing Page from Ben George's Portfolio

18

CHENGSU CHEN'S PORTFOLIO

Website URL: https://www.chengsuchen.com/

Website Builder: Wix

Keyword
- Standard
- Structured

Color
- #FFFFFF
- #1C1C1C
- #0152FF

Main Heading Font
- Font Family: Poppins
- Font Weight: Semi-bold
- Font Size: 1.2 rem
- Line Height: 1.12

Body Text Font
- Font Family: Work Sans
- Font Weight: Extra-light
- Font Size: 1 rem
- Line Height: 1.4

~

HOMEPAGE

Top Navigation Bar
- About
- Resume

Structure
- Short Bio
- Case Study 1
- Case Study 2
- Case Study 3
- Case Study 4
- Case Study 5

Visuals
- Creative typography
- Special logo

~

CASE STUDY PAGE

Structure
- Project Overview
  - *About*
  - *Duration*
  - *How the product works*
- People Problem
- Features
- Vision
- Goals
- Current Experience
- UXR Findings
- MVP
- Final Polish
  - *Walkthrough 1*
  - *Walkthrough 2*
- Experiment Results
- Hypotheses
- Proposed Solution
- Results
- Learnings

Visuals
- Two-column layout with text on the left and visuals on the right.
- Full-width sections with center-aligned text make the web page more dynamic.

~

SPECIAL SAUCE

- Case studies follow a standard storytelling structure that is easy to digest.
- "What I do in my free time" on the About page adds more personality.

Homepage from Chengsu Chen's Portfolio

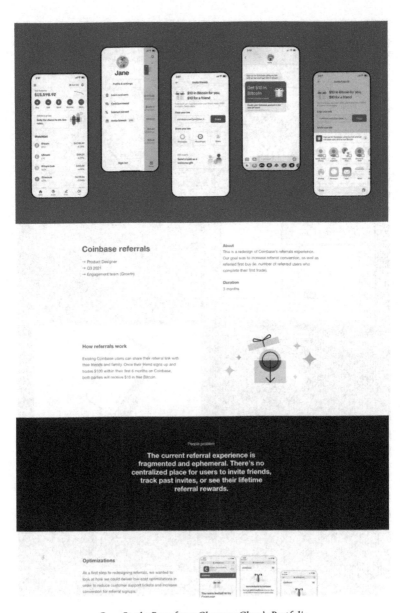

Case Study Page from Chengsu Chen's Portfolio

About Page from Chengsu Chen's Portfolio

19

MIRANDA WONG'S PORTFOLIO

Website URL: https://mirandacwong.com/

Website Builder: Hand-coded

Keyword
- Elegant
- Interactive
- Thoughtful

Color
- #FFFBF3
- #F8F9F9

Main Heading Font
- Font Family: Swear Display
- Font Weight: Light
- Font Size: 1.5 rem
- Line Height: 1.2

Body Text Font
- Font Family: Inter
- Font Weight: Regular
- Font Size: 1 rem
- Line Height: 1.5

HOMEPAGE

Top Navigation Bar
- Home
- About
- After Hours
- Resume

Structure
- Case Study 1
- Case Study 2
- Case Study 3
- Case Study 4
- Case Study 5
- For Me, Design Is

Visuals
- Hover effects—image reveal, cursor change, and drop shadow.
- Auto-rotating element—"Let's build something together".
- The clear visual hierarchy between titles and

descriptions.
- The application of small, delightful icons.

∾

CASE STUDY PAGE

Structure
- Project Details
  - *My Role*
  - *Team*
  - *Duration*
  - *Tools*
- Project Overview
- UX Research
- Research Synthesis
- Illustrating Experiences
- Low-fidelity Concepts
- UI Refinement
- Gathering feedback - Round 1
- Gathering feedback - Round 2
- Final Designs
- Demos
- My Learnings

Visuals
- Two-column layout: section titles on the left; body text and images on the right.
- Divider lines between sections to help break up the content.

~

SECRET SAUCE

- The comprehensive About page adds more
  personality and demonstrates her point of view
  as a designer.

Nice to meet you, I'm *Miranda*. I'm a *product designer* and *illustrator* based in the *SF Bay Area* working toward some kind of world betterment. ☺

Recently graduated with a degree in both Design and Managerial Economics from the University of California, Davis.

Currently designing and rethinking the student experience in higher education at Workday.

Illustrating and running a small stationery shop on the side.

Welcome
↓

FreeBites

Fall 2020

Improving and extending the food sharing experience to the larger community ↗

UX Design, UI Design

Homepage from Miranda Wong's Portfolio

UI refinement   We presented our low-fidelity concepts in our first design review with our client and were able to confirm development feasibility and approval of each of our solutions.

Building a moodboard   We put together a moodboard for inspiration before creating our own design system.

Establishing a design system   Once we felt we were in agreement with the visual feel, we decided on a design system to ensure consistency across all screens and ease the development process.

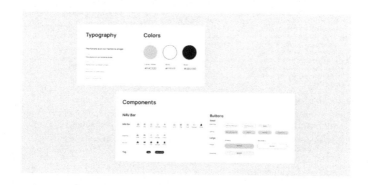

Part I: Gathering feedback   As a team we polished up the screens that would be used in user testing and established our main user testing goals.

Questions to answer   1. How effortless is it to complete tasks pertaining to each of the 3 user types?

     2. How well does our assumed user flow align with our users' approach?

Case Study Page from Miranda Wong's Portfolio

Appreciate you taking the extra step to get to know me!

a little more about me 🐚 ↑

first things first

I'm Miranda, a recent graduate from UC Davis with a dual degree in Design and Business Economics. Go Ags :')

personal endeavors

I'm volunteering as a product designer at OpenMeal, non-profit organization dedicated to serving meals to those in need while also supporting local restaurants! I'm very drawn to volunteer opportunities that aid and serve underserved communities and those who need support in crises.

currently!

I'm an Associate Product Designer working on the Student Design team at Workday. I'm so grateful for this opportunity and I'm excited to learn and grow in this new role!

for me, design is ✳ ↑

compassion

I think deeply about the stories of the people who will use my designs and the context of their experience.

like building a home

A home must go beyond being functional and a space for fulfilling our basic needs. The same applies to design. Good design delivers comfort, beauty, and a sense of identity.

never just work

Design is more than just work. It enables us to explore, experiment, and equip ourselves with novel ways of taking on challenges in the real world.

after hours ☽ ↑

the alexas

At the start of quarantine, a couple of friends and I started a band and we called ourselves, The Alexas! Singing was a thing confined within my shower walls, but this band has given me a space to explore, make mistakes, and trust myself — things that now heavily support me in my design career.

my Etsy shop

I'm an illustrator on the side running my own Etsy shop! I started my journey as a visual designer and this has been my avenue to continue focusing on craft and creative vision. Find my work here and here :')

thrifting + spending time with my family

Clothes that were pre-loved are the most special to me, especially the ones handed down to me from my parents and grandparents. If I'm not thrifting, I'm spending some quality time with my family!

design resources ✦ ↑

getting started

Bestfolios for portfolio inspiration
The Guide to Design
Bite Size UX

new perspectives

UX Collective
Julie Zhuo for the best advice
Joey Banks

keep learning

Something to learn each day

support your local community + abroad ✳ ↑

aapi

Heart of Dinner
Chinese Food Club
Asian Veggies
Welcome to Chinatown

blm

A Growing List of Resources
Want to donate?

abroad

War in Ukraine
Afghanistan Matters

About Page from Miranda Wong's Portfolio

SF Bay Area working
toward some kind of
world betterment. ☻

Appreci_____ ___ __ step to get

a little more about me ⊛

About Page from Miranda Wong's Portfolio

20

BUZZ USBORNE'S PORTFOLIO

Website URL: https://buzzusborne.com/

Website Builder: Hand-coded

Keyword
- Creative
- Delightful
- Whimsical

Color
- #FFFFFF
- #14243C
- #874BF7

Main Heading Font
- Font Family: Raleway
- Font Weight: Bold
- Font Size: 2 rem

- Line Height: 1

Body Text Font
- Font Family: Roboto
- Font Weight: Regular
- Font Size: 1 rem
- Line Height: 2

HOMEPAGE

Top Navigation Bar
- Home
- Work
- About
- Coaching

Structure
- Bio
- Work
  - *Case Study 1*
  - *Case Study 2*
  - *Case Study 3*
  - *Case Study 4*
  - *Case Study 5*
  - *Case Study 6*
  - *Case Study 7*
  - *Case Study 8*
  - *Case Study 9*

- Other Work

Visuals
- Creative hover interaction
- Pleasant visual details
- Well-designed card thumbnails
- Elegant signature as website logo and favicon

CASE STUDY PAGE

Structure
- Summary
- My Role
- Creative Direction
- Feature Work

Visuals
- Large, high-quality user interface designs.
- Single-column layout with shorter line lengths.
- Creative divider lines.

~

SPECIAL SAUCE

- Strong visual craft demonstrated in UI and portfolio design.
- A wide range of projects showcasing his extensive experience in design.
- Authentic, personal storytelling.

Hey, I'm Buzz, a UX & UI Designer with 19+ years creative experience and a passion for designing collaborative products that customers love to use. I coach designers, build tools that enable teams to work more effectively, and create the tools that help companies scale.

See my work...

Homepage from Buzz Usborne's Portfolio

Designing carbon calculators to AI support tools...

I've been hard at work producing UI for a range of companies... from document signing to customer support and environmental compliance tools.

Coming soon...

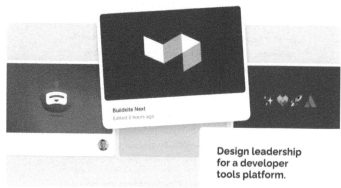

Design leadership for a developer tools platform.

Software used by engineering teams all over the world to test, fix and ship their code. Bringing insight, fun and humanity to an industry built around code.

View

A chat app that helps connect humans.

I created a whole new product channel for Help Scout customers to talk directly with their own customers — a way to connect humans, not bots.

Work Page from Buzz Usborne's Portfolio

Buildkite

SUMMARY

Buildkite is a tool used by the world's biggest software teams like Uber, Airbnb and Canva to securely test and deploy their code. I led the design team as the company scaled, helping build human-friendly solutions to tough technical problems.

My role at Buildkite was to build Design into a high-performing asset of the business — I did that by building creative strategy, establishing effective team processes and producing visual work that helped us scale our product footprint.

Team time!

Great design doesn't happen in isolation. To unlock success in our small but extremely capable creative team, I created a variety of tools and processes that helped the team communicate and collaborate more effectively. Importantly, I worked hard to prioritize creativity and professional development. Ultimately, I ended up writing a heap...

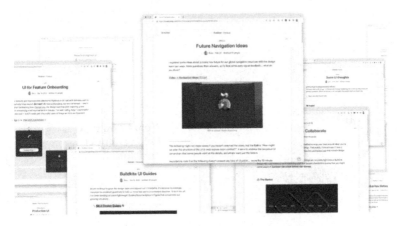

Case Study Page from Buzz Usborne's Portfolio

I was a competitive sailor and coach before designing for a living. I taught all ages and abilities whilst also participating in several internationally recognized events. My mind is never too far from the ocean, and I appreciate the importance of a healthy work/life balance. So when I'm not online, you'll find me outside with my wife... chasing my two kids, swimming, running or riding motorbikes.

~~~~~~~

🎤 Speaking

I'm privileged to have been invited to talk at a number of events about design and my career. My aim is always to demystify the design process and encourage leaning into discomfort. I talk about building small but effective design teams, how to keep creativity alive, and how to grow your career as a designer. I only talk at events where my experience is unique and additive, and where I can be part of a diverse lineup.

Events

- The Truth About Design Leadership — WDX Conf, 2023
- Encouraging Creativity — Vero Conf, 2023
- Adapt & Grow — Edge of the Web Conference, 2022
- Influencing Work as a Designer — Domain, 2022

About Page from Buzz Usborne's Portfolio

21

MICHAEL LO'S PORTFOLIO

Website URL: https://www.vvichael.com/

Website Builder: Webflow

Keyword
- Minimalist
- Clean
- Sleek

Color
- #FFFFFF
- #F3F3F3
- #161616

Main Heading Font
- Font Family: Leitura News
- Font Weight: Regular
- Font Size: 1.7 rem

- Line Height: 1.25

Body Text Font
- Font Family: Söhne
- Font Weight: Regular
- Font Size: 1 rem
- Line Height: 1.6

HOMEPAGE

Top Navigation Bar
- Work
- Info

Structure
- Short Bio
- Case Study 1
- Case Study 2
- Case Study 3
- Case Study 4
- Case Study 5
- Other Projects

Visuals
- Extra large project thumbnails with small text.
- High-quality, sleek visual mockups.

~

CASE STUDY PAGE

Structure
- Project Overview
  - *Client*
  - *Contribution*
  - *Team*
  - *Project Introduction*
- Challenge 1
- Solution
- Challenge 2
- Solution
- Challenge 3
- Solution

Visuals
- Full-width, high-quality user interface designs.
- Single-column layout for text with optimized line lengths for readability.
- Light gray color as the image background to break the long page into chunks.

~

SPECIAL SAUCE

- Extra-large visuals highlight strong craft in design.
- Great balance between text and visuals, ensuring great readability.

Homepage from Michael Lo's Portfolio

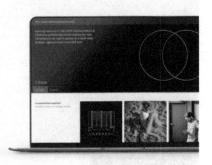

IBM **C.School** is a learning platform that helps IBM's Communication and Citizenship professionals further develop their core competencies and skills.

Client
IBM Communication
Jun 2019 – Dec 2019

Contribution
User Experience

Team
Annette Cheung, Max Castain, Jason
Neil Hyekyung, Marielle Peterson, Sean
Nguyen

IBM C.School
A learning platform designed for IBM
Communication & Citizenship
professionals

Case Study Page from Michael Lo's Portfolio

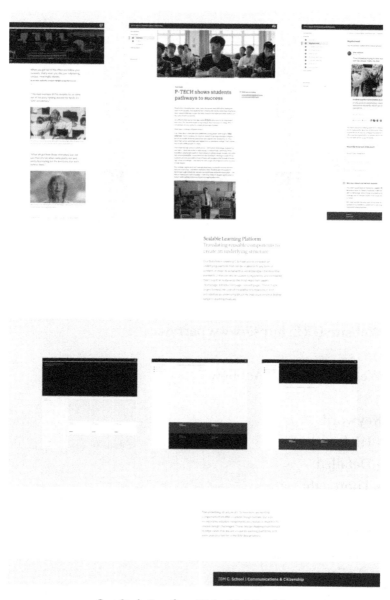

Case Study Page from Michael Lo's Portfolio

22

PERRY WANG'S PORTFOLIO

Website URL: https://www.perryw.ca/

Website Builder: Webflow

Keyword
- High-tech
- Detailed
- Thorough

Color
- #101010
- #F2F2F2
- #979797

Main Heading Font
- Font Family: PP Neue Montreal
- Font Weight: Medium
- Font Size: 1.5 rem

- Line Height: 1.25

Body Text Font
- Font Family: PP Neue Montreal
- Font Weight: Book
- Font Size: 1 rem
- Line Height: 1.5

HOMEPAGE

Top Navigation Bar
- Work
- Info
- LinkedIn
- Resume

Structure
- Short Bio
- Case Study 1
- Case Study 2
- Case Study 3
- Case Study 4

Visuals
- Uncommon dark-themed website.
- Subtle animated effects above the fold.
- White and gray text to establish visual hierarchy.

~

CASE STUDY PAGE

Structure
- Project Information
  - *My Role*
  - *Team*
  - *Timeline & Status*
  - *Overview*
- Context
- The Problem
- Design Principles
- Discovery
- Layout
- Interactions
- Visual Design
- Final Designs
- Retrospective

Visuals
- In-depth visual details, including callouts and specifications.
- A wide range of animated prototypes to explain the design.

~

SPECIAL SAUCE

- The attractive website design demonstrates his strong visual acumen.
- The in-depth storytelling walks through the whole design process.
- The "Friends" section on the About page includes links to other portfolios.

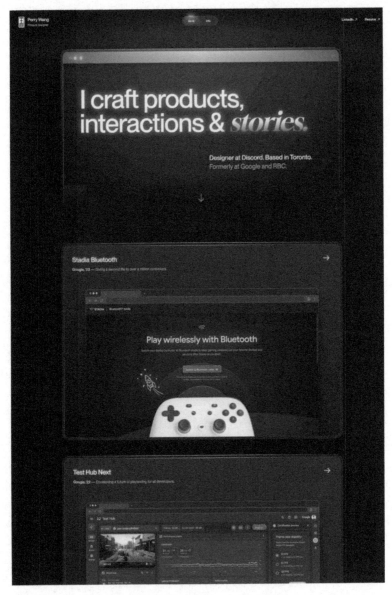

Homepage from Perry Wang's Portfolio

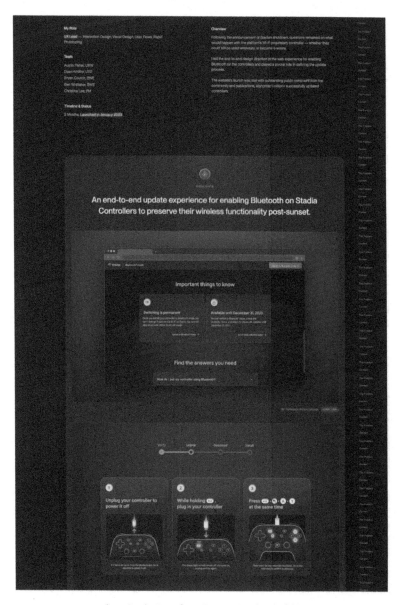

Case Study Page from Perry Wang's Portfolio

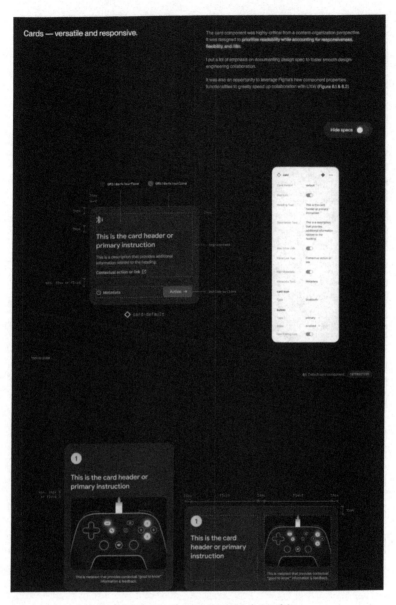

Case Study Page from Perry Wang's Portfolio

23

TAMMY TAABASSUM'S PORTFOLIO

Website URL: https://taamannae.dev/

Website Builder: Hand-coded

Keyword
• Comprehensive
• Well-rounded
• Thoughtful

Color
• #FFFFFF
• #000000

Main Heading Font
• Font Family: Manrope
• Font Weight: Extra-light
• Font Size: 2.22 rem
• Line Height: 1.2

Body Text Font

- Font Family: Manrope
- Font Weight: Extra-light
- Font Size: 1 rem
- Line Height: 1.5

❧

HOMEPAGE

Top Navigation Bar

- Work
- My Design Process
- Freelance
- Fun
- Articles
- About
- Resume

Structure

- Bio
- Case Study 1
- Case Study 2
- Case Study 3
- Case Study 4
- Case Study 5
- Case Study 6
- Case Study 7
- Case Study 8
- Case Study 9

- Case Study 10
- Visuals
- Animated personal fun facts

~

CASE STUDY PAGE

Structure
- Project Information
  - *Role*
  - *Timeline*
  - *Tools*
- Overview
  - Problem
  - Outcome
- End Result
  - *Showcase 1*
  - *Showcase 2*
  - *Showcase 3*
  - *Showcase 4*
  - *Showcase 5*
- Setting Expectation
- Uncovering Issues
- Ideation
- Mid-Fi
- Testing & Iterations
- Branding
- A New Logo
- Creating Consistency

- Final Design
- Lessons Learned

Visuals
- Alternated color backgrounds to improve the readability of long pages.
- Clear section headings with numbers and lines.

～

SPECIAL SAUCE

- The Fun page shows her creative explorations.
- The Freelance page highlights her experience as an engineer turned product designer.

Hello! I'm Tammy,
I write medium articles about design

I am a product designer & front-end engineer with some illustration chops. I have a wide range of experience from big tech and agency to and startups. Co-Founder @ Octoshop. Incoming @ Figma. Previously @ *Meta, Xbox & Wish*

It's nice to meet you, check out my work below

Work   001

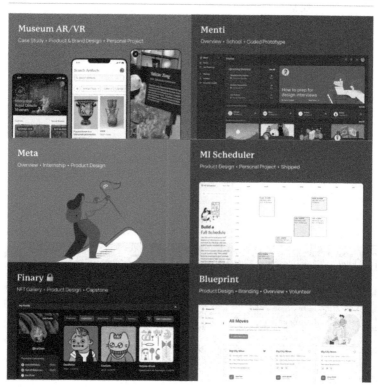

Homepage from Tammy Taabassum's Portfolio

Project   001   Info   003

ROM

A mobile app and AR/VR
experience to make the Royal
Ontario Museum *more engaging*

I've always been interested in emerging technology. As a way to improve my skills, I decided to learn VR/AR prototyping and design. I made this experience as a personal project to improve these skills and get better as a designer. Current museum experiences are stagnant and many people find they lack engagement. Living Museum brings the past alive through interactive and immersive stories. Users can see how artifacts are connected, their stories, fun facts, and their histories. **This project is not affiliated with the Royal Ontario Museum in Toronto. It is just for practice.**

Role
Product Designer

Timeline
Jan 2022 - April 2022

Tools
Figma
Unity
Google Suite

Overview   002

Problem
How might we make museum experiences more immersive, exciting, and story-driven?

Outcome
I created a web, mobile AR and Unity VR experience that makes digital museum visits more fun through scavenger hunts, personal collection curation and immersive exhibits

End Result   004

Final application
designs & solutions

Over the course of 4 months, I worked on a multimodal experience for museum experiences. This included building desktop, mobile, AR, VR applications and a design system that supports all it. This project aims to make museum experience **more immersive & interactive.**

Case Study Page from Tammy Taabassum's Portfolio

Fun Page from Tammy Taabassum's Portfolio

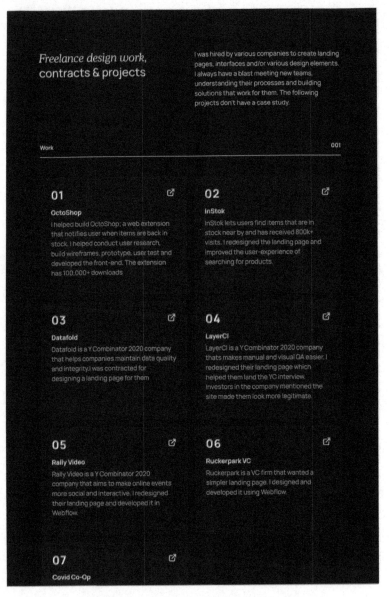

Freelance design work,
contracts & projects

I was hired by various companies to create landing pages, interfaces and/or various design elements. I always have a blast meeting new teams, understanding their processes and building solutions that work for them. The following projects don't have a case study.

Work   001

01

OctoShop

I helped build OctoShop; a web extension that notifies user when items are back in stock. I helped conduct user research, build wireframes, prototype, user test and developed the front-end. The extension has 100,000+ downloads

02

InStok

InStok lets users find items that are in stock near by and has received 800k+ visits. I redesigned the landing page and improved the user-experience of searching for products.

03

Datafold

Datafold is a Y Combinator 2020 company that helps companies maintain data quality and integrity.I was contracted for designing a landing page for them

04

LayerCI

LayerCI is a Y Combinator 2020 company thats makes manual and visual QA easier. I redesigned their landing page which helped them land the YC interview. Investors in the company mentioned the site made them look more legitimate.

05

Rally Video

Rally Video is a Y Combinator 2020 company that aims to make online events more social and interactive. I redesigned their landing page and developed it in Webflow.

06

Ruckerpark VC

Ruckerpark is a VC firm that wanted a simpler landing page. I designed and developed it using Webflow.

07

Covid Co-Op

Freelance Page from Tammy Taabassum's Portfolio

24

SIMON PAN'S PORTFOLIO

Website URL: https://simonpan.com/

Website Builder: WordPress

Keyword
- Thorough
- Classic
- Narrative

Color
- #FFFFFF
- #252B33
- #F5F6F7
- #B51A18
- #E9EDEF

Main Heading Font
- Font Family: Bebas Neue

- Font Weight: Bold
- Font Size: 2.3 rem
- Line Height: 1.3

Body Text Font
- Font Family: Calluna
- Font Weight: Light
- Font Size: 1 rem
- Line Height: 1.5

HOMEPAGE

Top Navigation Bar
- Portfolio
- Writing
- About

Structure
- Case Study 1
- Case Study 2
- Case Study 3

Visuals
- Success metrics are included in the project thumbnails.

~

CASE STUDY PAGE

Structure
- Project Overview
  - *Context*
  - *The Challenge*
  - *My Role*
  - *Kickoff*
  - *The Discovery*
  - *Deep Insights*
  - *Reframing the Problem*
- The Redesign
- How We Got There
  - *Design Strategies*
  - *Possible Concepts*
  - *Design Challenges*
  - *Data Insights*
  - *Discovery, Design Iterations, and Testing*
- The Launch
- The Impact

Visuals
- Alternated color backgrounds—white, gray, and black.
- Short paragraphs with large fonts and short line lengths.
- Strong typographic hierarchy with headings (bold, all-caps) and pull quotes (red, center-aligned).

~

SPECIAL SAUCE

- The comprehensive, thoughtful storytelling has made his portfolio a classic.

PORTFOLIO
WRITING
ABOUT

UBER MAGIC 2.0

Led redesign of the pickup experience to launch the Uber Rider App 2.0. Reduced average driver wait-time (-20%) and pickup error distance (-34%).

Read More

AMAZON PRIME MUSIC

Led design of Prime Music service launch on iOS and Android. Increased monthly active days per user (+50%), monthly listening hours per user (+36%) and new customer retention rate (+31%).

Read More

LONDON BY BIKE

Led redesign of the Barclays Cycle Hire app – featured in the App Store's Top 20 free travel apps

Read More

INDEPENDENT LIVING NSW

Led redesign of 'AT Magic' webapp to assist Health Professionals provide care for their clients. Increased active monthly users (+218%).

Read More

simon.pan@live.com · Twitter · LinkedIn · Dribbble · Buy me a coffee

Website design and content © 2014 Simon Pan

Homepage from Simon Pan's Portfolio

145

FREQUENT CONTACT TO CONFIRM OR COORDINATE LOCATION

Riders were annoyed when they were contacted by their Driver to confirm the location. Riders expected Uber to do the work and didn't feel the need to reiterate.

SUBOPTIMAL ROUTES GIVEN TO DRIVER

Riders were frustrated with the specific routes that the Driver used in getting to their pickup location. Riders expected Uber routing to be smarter.

UNEXPECTED ARRIVAL LOCATION

Often, Drivers did not arrive where the Rider expected. Riders would need to cross the road, backtrack on the block or negotiate an alternative pickup location.

PIN SETTERS AND BUTTON MASHERS

Riders behave in two distinct ways. Those who explicitly set a pickup location (via search or pin) and those that expected the Driver to arrive at their current location.

THE DISCOVERY

RIDER EXPECTATIONS CHANGED OVER TIME

I was surprised by the issues we found. They felt like privileged San Francisco annoyances, rather than major problems faced by our global audience. But after some thinking, it became clearer that Riders expected the experience to just work with minimal effort. As Uber became more integral to their lives, their expectations evolved.

Case Study Page from Simon Pan's Portfolio

WORKING BACKWARDS FROM PERFECT

Before I could jump into designing, it was important to define success and understand the health of the pickup experience at scale.

Prior to the redesign, *contact rate* i.e the rate at which a phone call occurs during the pickup was the only proxy we had used to measure pickup quality.

I unpacked the concept of the *perfect pickup* and modeled for the dimensions of time, space and anxiety.

I partnered with our data scientist and used this framework to investigate the pickup health around the world.

Goal	Signal	Metric
The pickup occurred	Cancellations	Rider cancellation rate, Driver cancellation rate, Completion rate
The pickup experience as good	Anxiety and stress, satisfaction	Rider NPS, Rider satisfaction, Driver NPS, Driver satisfaction
The pickup occurred at specified location	Distance between specified location and actual location	Pickup location error, High precision pickups, Low precision pickups
The pickup occurred at specified time	Estimated time of arrival, forecasted time to destination, Driver lateness, Rider lateness, Major trip problems	ETA prediction accuracy, On-time arrival rate, Mean arrival time error, Late arrival rate, Early arrival rate, Post-arrival waiting time
The pickup occurred effortlessly	Walking distance, Driver circling, Rider rendezvousing, communication overhead	Walking distance, Average zero pickup rate, contact rate, Multi contact rate, Contact duration

MOST PICKUPS REQUIRE ADDITIONAL PHYSICAL OR COORDINATION EFFORT

Digging into the data revealed some big insights into the pickup experience. Almost all trips involved some extra *coordination effort* such as a phone call to clarify the location and additional *physical effort* such as walking somewhere else to meet the driver, or the driver re-circling the block. This data showed that the experience was hardly the *door-to-door magic* Uber had been optimized for.

> "In a city as busy as San Francisco, over \$1 million was wasted per week because of problematic pickups."

The time and energy spent recovering during problematic pickup situations was having a material impact on the business bottom line. Waiting time translates directly into network under-utilization and every phone call costs to anonymize.

In a city like San Francisco, over \$1 million was wasted per week because of problematic pickups. Cities like Guangzhou and New Delhi were much worse.

Case Study Page from Simon Pan's Portfolio

25

SEÁN HALPIN'S PORTFOLIO

Website URL: https://www.seanhalpin.xyz/

Website Builder: Hand-coded

Keyword:
- Sleek
- Interactive
- Delightful

Color:
- #EEE7DE
- #04594D

Main Heading Font:
- Font Family: Acorn
- Font Weight: Semi-bold
- Font Size: 2 rem
- Line Height: 1.3

Body Text Font:
- Font Family: GT Planar
- Font Weight: Regular
- Font Size: 1 rem
- Line Height: 1.6

~

HOMEPAGE

Top Navigation Bar
- Work
- About
- Play
- Notes
- Contact

Structure
- Short Bio
- Case Study 1
- Case Study 2
- Case Study 3
- Case Study 4
- Work in Progress

Visuals
- Prominent headline with large text, artistic font, and icons.
- Animated color background above the fold.
- Thoughtfully designed project thumbnails with consis-

tent styles and hover interactions.

～

CASE STUDY PAGE

Structure
- Project Information
  - *Timeline*
  - *Team*
  - *Role*
- Overview
- Exploration
- Other Applications

Visuals
- High-quality, animated prototypes.
- Creative hover interactions.
- Great balance between text and visuals.
- Short paragraphs that are easy to read.

～

SPECIAL SAUCE

- The Play page shows a variety of creative side projects that he designed and developed.

- Delightful visual and interaction design details are presented across the website.

Homepage from Seán Halpin's Portfolio

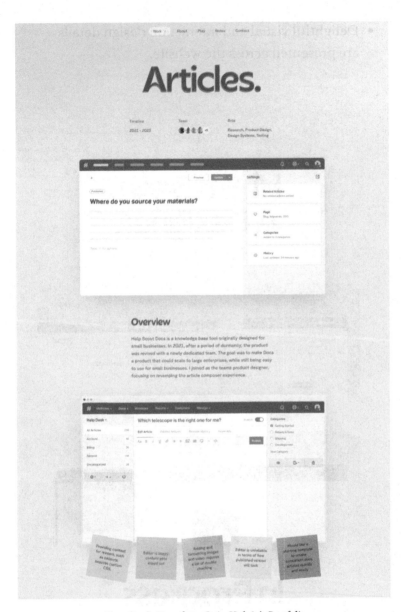

Case Study Page from Seán Halpin's Portfolio

I'm Seán.

I'm a Product Designer working remotely from 15°C Dublin, Ireland.

Over the past 12+ years, I've worked in various areas of digital design, including front-end development, email, marketing, and app UI/UX. I'm proud to have worn many hats.

These days, I focus on leading design at GiveDirectly, a nonprofit that lets donors send money directly to the world's poorest households.

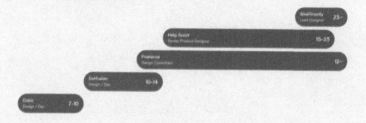

Let's collaborate if you're committed to sustainability, education, equality, or carbon neutrality.

I believe we should leave this Earth as good as or better than we found it for future generations; my goal is to contribute to those ideals in whatever way I can. If you feel the same, I'd love to talk.

01

Make it

I sketch wireframes and make prototypes. Talking through tactile designs existing in the browser is worth its weight. Design tools only carry you so far; the rest should be realized with a link my team can rally around.

02

Collaborate

Good design is not created in a vacuum but rather in a shared space. It must be facilitated and iterated upon as a team. I aim to include stakeholders in my design process and create a collaborative environment that welcomes and encourages feedback.

03

Accessible FTW

I aim to make everything I design accessible to all for one main reason - it's the right thing to do. Accessible products benefit the many, not the few.

04

Keep experimenting

Everything I create is subject to change and experimentation. Not everything will work, but it's worth trying - and learning from what doesn't.

About Page from Seán Halpin's Portfolio

26

AILEEN SHIN'S PORTFOLIO

Website URL: https://www.aileen.co/

Website Builder: Hand-coded

Keyword
- Clean
- Thoughtful
- Narrative

Color
- #FFFFFF
- #323649

Main Heading Font
- Font Family: Charter ITC
- Font Weight: Bold
- Font Size: 1.75 rem
- Line Height: 1.3

Body Text Font
- Font Family: Apercu
- Font Weight: Regular
- Font Size: 1 rem
- Line Height: 1.6

~

HOMEPAGE

Top Navigation Bar
- Work
- Info

Structure
- Short Bio
- Case Study 1
- Case Study 2
- Case Study 3
- Case Study 4
- Case Study 5
- Case Study 6
- Case Study 7

Visuals
- Minimalist design with concise text and simple project thumbnails.

~

CASE STUDY PAGE

Structure
- Project Overview
  - *Role*
  - *Timeline*
- More Context
- Original Experience
- Project Goals
  - *User & Business Goals*
  - *Definition of Success*
- Challenge
  - *Challenge 1 (How Might We)*
  - *Challenge 2 (How Might We)*
  - *Challenge 3 (How Might We)*
- Design Explorations
- Iterating & Validating Assumptions
- Final Design
  - *Highlight 1*
  - *Highlight 2*
  - *Highlight 3*
- Impact
- Team

Visuals
- Large, full-width visual mockups.
- Sufficient white space on the page.
- Different section backgrounds—white, gray, and dotted.

~

SPECIAL SAUCE

- A variety of visuals is used—3D UI mockups, enlarged callouts, and creative placements of images.

Aileen is a digital product designer living in ~~Berlin~~
Seattle

Tumblr — Making Queueing Better on Mobile
Product Design

Edenspiekermann — Designing a Shared Transportation Experience
Product Design, Agency

Unique Board — Empowering Creative Collaboration
Product Design, Startups

General Assembly — Improving Student Engagement
User Research, Strategy

General Assembly — Designing SQL Challenges
Product Design, UI Animation

Homepage from Aileen Shin's Portfolio

Tumblr

Tumblr is the foremost place where close-knit communities share their new ideas, new passions, and new forms of self-expression.

This is an internship project I worked on during my time at Tumblr as an intern on Tumblr's Product Design team of four designers. From research, UX, visual design, and prototyping, I was fortunate to own the problem, lead the project with the help of the team, and ship the feature in September 2016 on the Google Play Store.

The nature of posting on Tumblr

Posting on Tumblr is different from posting on other social networks because users aren't encouraged to say who they are, but just to share what they love. It allows them to build a collage of their passion no matter their identity.

During a user study, I chatted with Jen, a power user of seven years, and watched her reblog three posts in less than five minutes for two of her Tumblr blogs. When I asked what motivates her to post on Tumblr, she said posting feels lighter since the posts aren't directly tied to her identity.

Tumblr is designed so that users can post as many as 250 posts a day whether it's creating an original post or reblogging a post. This unique nature of posting allows users to publish a post in many different ways: users can schedule a post for a specific time, save it as a draft, post it privately, or add it to queue.

Queueing posts helps blogs grow even when users are away

The queue keeps users' blog actively posting and growing even when they're at school, work, or sleeping.

Users can set how many posts get published automatically during a specific time frame of a day.

Case Study Page from Aileen Shin's Portfolio

Iterating & Validating Assumptions

After loops of feedback and weekly design critiques from the Product
Design team and the Engineering team, we learned that design
treatments that are native Material Design would drive greater
efficiency and create more coherent experience for users.

We also worked closely with the Copy team to shape and polish the
product experience. The Copy team played a significant role by
crafting clear, friendly copy that helps users achieve a goal and
understand the value of queueing.

We continued to collaborate with teams for feedback. Validating our
design solutions through user testing especially helped to become
confident in our design decisions.

Case Study Page from Aileen Shin's Portfolio

27

JESS CHEN'S PORTFOLIO

Website URL: https://www.jesschen.com/

Website Builder: Hand-coded

Keyword
- Sleek
- Elegant
- Sophisticated

Color
- #FFFFFF
- #17206E
- #333333

Main Heading Font
- Font Family: Montserrat
- Font Weight: Thin
- Font Size: 1 rem

- Line Height: 1.2

Body Text Font
- Font Family: Nunito
- Font Weight: Extra-light
- Font Size: 1 rem
- Line Height: 1.375

HOMEPAGE

Top Navigation Bar
- Work
- Resume
- About

Structure
- Short Bio
- Case Study 1
- Case Study 2
- Case Study 3
- Case Study 4
- Case Study 5
- More Bio
  - Talking Points
  - Work Experience
  - Education
  - Social Media
  - Contact

Visuals

• The About page is essentially the button section of the Homepage.

• The minimalist design with fun copy adds personality.

~

CASE STUDY PAGE

Structure

• Background
• Research & Discovery
• Problem Statement
• Goals
• Wireframes
• User Testing & Discoveries
• Further Iterations
• User Testing
• Visual Design & Animations
• The Team

Visuals

• Sections with different color backgrounds.

• Full-width images, balanced with single-column text.

• A variety of visuals, including 3D UI mockups, collages, and compelling hand sketches.

~

SPECIAL SAUCE

- While succinct, the About section on the Homepage effectively conveys an engaging personality.

Hello!

My name is Jess and I'm a product designer.
I come from an industrial design background
and have worked on WiFi, social media,
jewelry, and toys.

JESS CHEN

// Talk to me (ie. talking points)

// See me on paper

// See me in the wild

TALKING POINTS

I write in all caps. Pilot G-Tec pens rock. Baking
helps to calm me. Once upon a time, I wanted to
be a vet. I love old people. Messiest desk in the
office, most organized Sketch files in the land bay.

WORK

July '19 - Present // Google
UX DESIGNER

Mar. '18 - June '19 // Facebook
PRODUCT DESIGNER

May '15 - Mar. '18 // oero
UX DESIGNER

Dec. '14 - Apr. '15 // Place
RESEARCH & UX DESIGN INTERN

June '14 - Sept. '14 // Nokia
INDUSTRIAL DESIGN INTERN

EDUCATION

University of Cincinnati
B.S. INDUSTRIAL DESIGN

Chiba University
EXCHANGE STUDENT

Homepage from Jess Chen's Portfolio

165

EERO SETUP 2.0
Improving WiFi one setup at a time

BACKGROUND

With the success of eero's first product, we sought to improve our existing work and introduce a new line of eeros. The First Time User Experience(FTUX) team came together and had a retrospective discussion on what went well and what could be improved for setup. Simultaneously, our brand marketing team was kicking off the rebranding of eero. They aimed to give eero a fuller, more complete visual language. Throughout this project, I worked closely with our senior visual designer, Delisa, to ensure that our setup redesign would incorporate and compliment the new brand and design system.

RESEARCH & DISCOVERY

// Journey Mapping
// Competitive Analysis
// Data Analysis
// Brainstorm Facilitation

Since the launch of the first product, we had heard plenty of feedback from reviewers, customers, fellow coworkers, and beta testers. I worked closely with my product manager, Jack, on pinpointing the key issues our existing customers were having. I lead journey mapping workshops with stakeholders and the other product designers to gain insight into our user's experience.

Jack and I also went through many of the setups for mesh routers that had newly come to market after eero's launch. We found that many were similar to ours but we took note of what made some experiences better. Lastly, we worked with our data analysis and customer experience teams to figure out where our users were having the most trouble.

Case Study Page from Jess Chen's Portfolio

With that insight, I worked with my product manager to rethink pre-setup education. We tossed around ideas such as additional information on the packaging QSG (quick start guide) or an informational carousel for fresh download app users. We conceptualized on how to communicate things that can be very technical and intimating into something that would be approachable and easy to comprehend.

FINAL WELCOME SEQUENCE

Case Study Page from Jess Chen's Portfolio

167

CONCLUSION

As we come to the conclusion of this book, I hope you've found helpful insights and inspiration from the tips and examples shared.

Now, it's time to turn your attention to your portfolio and consider how to elevate it further.

Keep in mind that your portfolio is the initial impression you make on hiring managers—it's the important gateway to receiving those interview invitations. However, landing interviews is just the beginning; there's still plenty to learn to truly shine during the interview process.

For additional guidance and resources, make sure to explore the offerings on my website. I've put together a range of resources aimed at helping you excel in your design career journey.

xinranma.com

Please also leave a message there. I'd love to hear from you.

Crafting your portfolio, much like other aspects of your design journey, requires a significant amount of learning, unlearning, and iterating.

However, every bit of effort you invest and every lesson you learn will contribute to your growth as a designer.

You've got this.

Xinran

THE MINIMALIST CAREER CHANGER

If you are an aspiring product designer, you will likely find another book of mine helpful: *The Minimalist Career Changer*.

- Both printed and Kindle versions are available on Amazon.
- PDF version is available on Gumroad: **xinranma.gumroad.com**.

That is a book that I wish had existed when I was switching careers to product design. It took me many months of trial and error, countless interviews, and over 100 coffee chats to learn these lessons. The book was the #1 Amazon Bestseller in multiple categories and received the Literary Titan Gold Book Award.

Inside, you'll find:

- My personal stories
- 5 mindsets to achieve more with less
- Frameworks to choose the right projects
- Tips on interviews, portfolios, and personal branding
- Step-by-step guides to building compelling case studies
- A roadmap to break into product design in 5 months or less
- And much more

CASE STUDY STORYTELLING

Case Study Storytelling is another book I wrote to help new product designers craft and present a compelling case study step by step.

- Both printed and Kindle versions are available on Amazon.
- PDF version is available on Gumroad: **xinranma.gumroad.com.**

A great case study presentation is the most important key to landing a great job as a product designer. It was also an area that I personally struggled the most. I wish there were practical and in-depth resources online about it. Storytelling in case studies is not just about telling a compelling story out of what you have. It's much more than that. It is a strategic tool that can help you stay focused, prioritize tasks, save time, and gain clarity.

This is probably the most comprehensive guide you can find on this topic.

Inside, you'll discover:

- The essence of case study storytelling.
- How to frame problems for case studies.
- How to craft and present compelling solutions.
- How to draft and incorporate various story components.
- How to tackle the overall structure of the presentation.
- How to plan your case study strategically and get better results.
- How to improve the visuals of your presentation.
- 8 common mistakes in case studies and how to avoid them.
- 5 tips to enhance verbal delivery.
- A Worksheet to craft a compelling story.

BEFORE YOU GO

If you enjoy reading this book, please leave a short review on Amazon. It would mean the world to me.

Visit the book's page, click "Write a customer review" and share your thoughts.

Your feedback helps other readers discover this book.

Thank you for your kind support!

Xinran

ABOUT THE AUTHOR

Xinran Ma is a product designer and mentor. He helped hundreds of people change careers through webinars and coffee chats. He is the author of *The Minimalist Career Changer* and *Case Study Storytelling*, a five-time recipient of the ADPList's Top 1% Mentor Award, and a guest lecturer at the University of Connecticut and Pratt Institute. His work has been featured in leading publications such as Designboom, UX Collective, ArchDaily, American Illustration, Society of Illustrators, 3x3 Magazine, and Bustler.

Made in the USA
Las Vegas, NV
13 November 2024

11718391R00108